US ARMY
Alphabet Book

HIS WE'LL DEFEND

UNITED STATES ARMY
1775

JERRY PALLOTTA ★ SAMMIE GARNETT ★ Illustrated by ROB BOLSTER

Charlesbridge

Thank you to Uncle Dom Mazzola, Uncle Bob Lewis, Uncle Larry Mazzola, Uncle Tony Pallotta, Uncle John Cronin, Uncle Vinnie DiGiovanni, and Uncle Nazz Mazzola. They all served proudly.—J. P.

Thank you to my family members who bravely served: Big Daddy-Victor Molinary, Deb Mullins, Russell O. Large, Jimmy F. White, Gary Harrell, and Chad Harrell. And to my friends who also proudly served: Matthew Buretz, Mark Bryant, Ken Cole Jr., Ken Cole Sr., David Hubbard, Stella Jones, Victor McCune, Neil Pallotta, Rosa Lee Shouse, and Ron Williams.—S. G.

A humble thank-you to all the men and women who have fought to protect the freedom we enjoy.—R. B.

The authors would like to thank Mark Abueg, Nick Arnio, Joseph R. Blanton, Paul Boyce, Vincent Brooks, Kristen V. Brunson, Mark Bryant, Matthew Buretz, Brad Casselbury, David L. Chebahtah, Ken Cole Jr., Ken Cole Sr., Donna Council, Gregory Daniel, Manuel Diemer, Z. Frank Hanner, Steve Harding, Chad Harrell, Gary Harrell, Jacqueline Hawe, Bill Herbert, Gilbert High, Stan Holloway, Clinton Housel, Erica Howard, Jamie Hubans, David Hubbard, Chris Hurst, LeRoy Jewell, Ken Kassens, Jill Kiah, Renee Klish, Lauren Lachner, Gordon Landale, Jose L. Lopez, Adam Luther, Austin Mansfield, Victor McCune, James T. Naylor, John Nettles, Neil Pallotta, Al Park, Don Randall, Monica M. Rogers, Dina D. Ruck, Pete Russo, Matthew J. Seelinger, Rosa Lee Shouse, Selene Sims, James M. Spaw, Donald Wagner, Bruce Zielsdorf, and Lauren L. Zimmer.

Published by Charlesbridge
9 Galen Street, Watertown, MA 02472
(617) 926-0329 • www.charlesbridge.com

Library of Congress Cataloging-in-Publication Data
Names: Pallotta, Jerry, author. | Garnett, Sammie, author. | Bolster, Rob, illustrator.
Title: US Army alphabet book / Jerry Pallotta and Sammie Garnett; illustrated by Rob Bolster.
Other titles: U.S. Army alphabet book
Description: Watertown, MA: Charlesbridge Publishing, [2021] | Audience: Ages 4–7 | Audience: Grades K–1 | Summary: "This alphabet book has something about the US Army for every letter."—Provided by publisher
Identifiers: LCCN 2020014304 (print) | LCCN 2020014305 (ebook) | ISBN 9781570919534 (hardcover) | ISBN 9781632897510 (ebook)
Subjects: LCSH: United States. Army—Juvenile literature. | Alphabet books—Juvenile literature. | English language—Alphabet—Juvenile literature.
Classification: LCC UA25 .P26 2021 (print) | LCC UA25 (ebook) | DDC 355.00973—dc23
LC record available at https://lccn.loc.gov/2020014304
LC ebook record available at https://lccn.loc.gov/2020014305

Printed in China
(hc) 10 9 8 7 6 5 4 3 2 1

Illustrations done in mixed media
Display type set in Rockwell by Monotype
Text type set in Memphis by Adobe Systems Inc.
Color separations and printing by 1010 Printing International Limited in Huizhou, Guangdong, China
Production supervision by Jennifer Most Delaney
Designed by Cathleen Schaad

Aa

A is for Army. What is an army? An army is a large number of soldiers organized, armed, and trained to protect a nation.

On June 14, 1775, the Continental Army was created under the command of George Washington. It eventually became the United States Army. It is the oldest branch of America's armed forces.

Bb

B is for Basic Combat Training. Newly enlisted men and women are called recruits. For ten fast and furious weeks, they undergo rigorous physical, mental, and weapons training. The recruits graduate with the skills and self-discipline to become US Army soldiers.

They start the day with "WAKE UP!" In the old days, a bugle sounded reveille, the army's wake-up call.

C is for Cavalry. The original US Cavalry consisted of troops trained to fight on horseback. Horses and mules pulled supply wagons and cannons. Today's army has replaced the horses with trucks, tanks, and mobile weapons. Modern technology is faster and more efficient, but the spirit of the old cavalry lives on.

Standing tall . . .
and looking good . . .

Oughta be
in Hollywood . . .

Sound off—one . . . two . . .
Sound off—three . . . four . . .

Dd

D is for Drill Sergeant. A drill sergeant's job is to train new recruits. Drill sergeants lead by example and teach pride in self, army, and country. The new soldiers stand up straight, clean their room, take orders, and are polite—a mother's dream come true.

Marching cadences motivate recruits to move in unison during repetitive tasks. The drill sergeant, often the cadence caller, sings the first line. The soldiers echo a response.

E is for Engineer. The military uses engineers in battle. They are called combat engineers. They fight alongside the infantry. Engineers are often out front, ready to remove obstacles and open supply routes. Here they are constructing an assault float bridge.

The mostly civilian US Army Corps of Engineers designs and builds public works projects—roads, buildings, monuments, harbors, and waterways.

Ee

F f

F is for Field Artillery. Field artillery is large weapons, huge guns, and missiles that require a crew to operate. Field artillery supports the infantry and armored units. Historically, field artillery is known as the King of Battle.

Gg

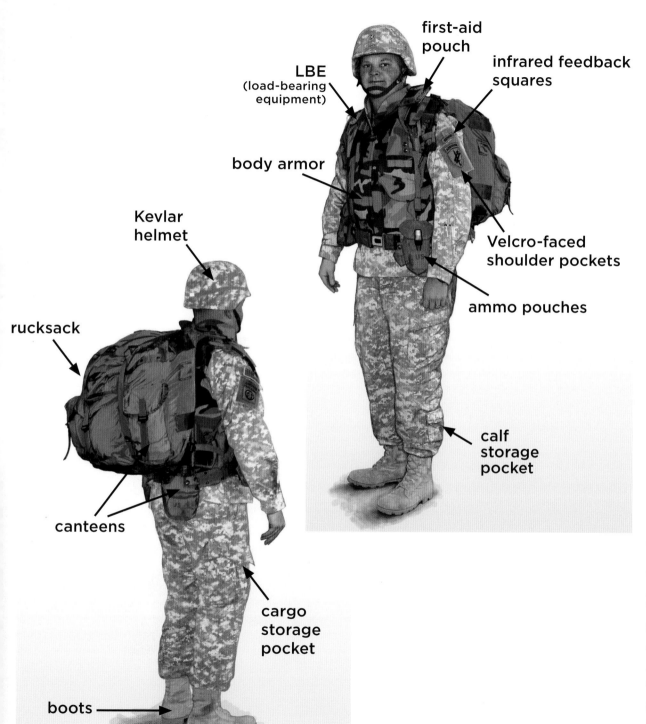

first-aid pouch

LBE (load-bearing equipment)

infrared feedback squares

body armor

Kevlar helmet

Velcro-faced shoulder pockets

rucksack

ammo pouches

canteens

calf storage pocket

cargo storage pocket

boots

G is for GI. More than one hundred years ago, supplies for the army were marked with the initials "GI," which stood for "government issue." As time passed, these initials came to be used for anything connected with the army. GI is a term for a soldier; a GI blanket is an army blanket; and to "GI it" means to clean something thoroughly.

Can you guess what this GI might carry? Batteries, earplugs, flashlight, ID card, notebook, pens, pocket knife, sewing kit, socks, toothbrush, whistle, waterproof matches, MREs (Meals, Ready-to-Eat), and chewing gum might all be found in a GI's rucksack.

Hh

H is for Helicopter. Jets, airplanes, and gliders are fixed-wing aircraft. Helicopters are rotary-wing aircraft. The spinning blades cause lift.

CHINOOK

LITTLE BIRD

Each US Army helicopter has a special job. The Chinook carries up to forty soldiers or heavy cargo. The Cayuse, also known as the Little Bird, is for special operations. The Kiowa is for scouting and spying.

KIOWA

The Black Hawk is a utility helicopter—it carries soldiers, weapons, and supplies. The Apache is an attack helicopter full of weapons. The Iroquois is a light utility helicopter.

BLACK HAWK

APACHE

IROQUOIS

Chopper is another word for helicopter. Battleships are named after states; aircraft carriers are named after presidents; and choppers are named after Native American tribes and people.

Ii

I is for Infantry. The infantry is the army's largest group of foot soldiers. It is also known as the Queen of Battle. The soldiers enter a battle zone on foot, in a vehicle, by parachute, or from a helicopter. The infantry's weapons have changed from bayonets and muzzle-loading muskets to automatic rifles, machine guns, night-vision laser scopes, rockets, and missiles.

Jj

J is for Jeep. The US Army started using jeeps during World War II. The jeep was a small, general-purpose vehicle. Because it was four-wheel drive and powerful, it was perfect for running errands, hauling soldiers, and undertaking reconnaissance missions.

No one knows for sure where the name "jeep" came from. It may have come from "general purpose," or "GP." Or it could be from a mischievous little character in Popeye cartoons named Jeep, who made only the sound *jeep*. He could go anywhere and do anything, which may have inspired the name. High Mobility Multipurpose Wheeled Vehicles, or Humvees, replaced jeeps in 1982.

Kk

K is for K-9 Corps. K-9 is a way of writing *canine*, which means "dog." The US Army has trained and worked with dogs since 1942. Dogs' loyalty and keen senses have saved the lives of many soldiers.

Sentry dogs patrol with guards and growl or bark if anyone approaches. Scout dogs silently detect snipers and other enemy forces. Messenger dogs carry information without being seen or heard. Casualty dogs help find wounded soldiers. Mine dogs perform the dangerous task of sniffing out bombs and booby traps.

L is for Logistics Support Vessel. The LSV is the army's largest powered watercraft. It can carry up to two thousand tons of cargo from a ship to the shore. With forward and aft ramps, the vessel has drive-through capability.

There are three types of LSVs: The LSV-HC, or helicopter carrier, transports helicopters or patrol boats hidden below the flight deck. The LSV-SSV, or semi-submersible variety, loads large floating cargo and patrol boats. The LSV-TC, or troop carrier, can carry 144 troops, six officers, supplies, and equipment.

Ll

Mm

M is for Medic. A medic is a soldier trained in emergency medicine. Medics are part of the medical corps that provides health care for the army. They are highly trained emergency medical technicians, or EMTs. In foreign countries, medics often treat local people. If an injured dog comes along, a medic will help it, too.

E5
Sergeant

E6
Staff Sergeant

E7
Sergeant
First Class

E8
First Sergeant /
Master Sergeant

E9
Sergeant Major /
Command
Sergeant Major

N is for Noncommissioned Officers. These dedicated professionals lead by example. Noncommissioned officers, or NCOs, provide outstanding leadership by knowing their soldiers, communicating with them, and treating them in a fair and impartial manner. NCOs are known as the Backbone of the Army.

Nn

O is for Officer. An army officer's most important duty is leadership. You can become a commissioned officer through the US Military Academy at West Point, the Army ROTC program, or Officer Candidate School. A good officer, just like the principal of your school, has command presence—when he or she enters a room, everyone pays attention.

Pp

P is for Paratrooper.
Paratroopers are infantry soldiers trained to parachute from an aircraft. They jump into combat zones in the daylight or darkness, carrying weapons and rucksacks, ready to fight as soon as they land.

Qq

Q is for Quartermaster Corps. The main mission of the Quartermaster Corps is to support the battlefield. Delivering supplies is their top responsibility. Supplies, supplies, and more supplies. They deliver food, water, clothing, fuel, personal items, and repair parts—anything a soldier needs. Sometimes the supplies arrive by aircraft through a "heavy drop."

R is for Reserves. Reservists are men and women from communities like yours who work in civilian jobs and train as soldiers one weekend each month plus two weeks each year. A firefighter in your town could be a helicopter pilot in the army! The army's citizen soldiers have always been ready to serve since the program began in 1908.

Rr

Ss

S is for Special Forces. In the US Army, special forces are called Green Berets. They are highly skilled soldiers trained in weapons, demolitions, engineering, communications, and medicine. They blend into foreign countries by learning the local language and culture. Green Berets are masters of unconventional warfare and counterinsurgency.

S is also for Special Operations. The 75th Ranger Regiment, also known as Army Rangers, is a special operations force. Rangers are the premier light, fast, flexible infantry unit. Rangers can attack by land, sea, or air—anywhere in the world—on short notice. They usually conduct raids and secure airfields at night with advanced weaponry and night-vision equipment.

Rangers are fast-roping down from these Black Hawks, and the sneaky Green Berets are already operating on the ground.

The army never acknowledges, talks, or writes about the special group called Delta Force. If someone tells you they are in Delta, they are not.

Tt

T is for Tomb Guards. Soldiers from the 3rd US Infantry Regiment, or the Old Guard, have been guarding the Tomb of the Unknown Soldier at Arlington National Cemetery since 1921. Guards are changed at the tomb every thirty minutes, twenty-four hours a day, every day of the year.

While on duty, a guard crosses a sixty-three-foot walkway in exactly twenty-one steps. They face the tomb for twenty-one seconds, turn again, and pause for twenty-one seconds before retracing their steps. Twenty-one is a symbolic number. It is the highest salute given to dignitaries in the military and at state ceremonies.

Continental Army

Union Army

World War I

World War II

Korean War

Vietnam War

Iraq and Afghanistan Wars

Uu

U is for Uniforms. US Army uniforms have told a story since soldiers began wearing them. They have changed with the times and will continue to change in years to come. A close look at a uniform helps identify when and where a soldier has served.

Vv

V is for Valor. The word *valor* means "bravery" or "courage." It is at the top of the Medal of Honor, which is the highest award for valor in combat. The Medal of Honor is the only US armed forces medal that is worn around the neck. There are Medal of Honor winners in every branch of service, and army personnel have been awarded the most.

W is for West Point. The West Point motto is "Duty, honor, country." The US Military Academy at West Point, New York, was established by Congress on March 16, 1802. It prepares young men and women to serve as officers in the US Army. Students are called cadets. They are issued a dress uniform and a hat called a tar bucket. The taller the feather on a senior's hat, the higher their rank. At the end of four years, cadets receive a bachelor of science degree and are commissioned as second lieutenants in the US Army.

Xx

X is for XM2010 Sniper Rifle. The *X* in its name means it is experimental. Soldiers test weapons in cold and hot weather, submerge them in water and mud, bury them in sand and dirt, and fire them multiple times to see if they fit army specifications. The XM2010 was officially adopted by the army in 2011 and lost its *X*, just like the other weapons on this page.

XM2010 Sniper Rifle,
first used 2010

M4 Carbine,
first used 1997

M240B Machine Gun,
first used 1997

M16 Rifle,
first used 1964

M249 Squad Automatic Weapon,
first used 1987

MK19-3 40mm Grenade Machine Gun,
first used 1983

M203/M203A-1 Grenade Launcher,
first used 1970s

Yy

Y is for You. Uncle Sam's recruiting posters say, "I WANT YOU FOR U.S. ARMY." They have hung in US Army recruiting offices since 1917. No one is certain how the character Uncle Sam was created. Over the years, he has come to symbolize the federal government of the United States.

Zz

Z is for Zodiac. Zodiac is the brand name of a CRRC—a combat rubber raiding craft. It can be launched from anywhere, even from a submarine.

This team started a raid by pumping up this inflatable boat. They attacked at night from an unsuspected location because a Zodiac offers no protection from small arms fire.

The US Navy has more ships, but the US Army has more boats.

UNITED STATES ARMY RANKS

ENLISTED SOLDIERS

Private E
(no insignia)

Private E-2

Private
First Class

Corporal

Specialist

Sergeant

Sergeant
Staff

Sergeant
First Class

Master
Sergeant

First
Sergeant

Sergeant
Major

Command
Sergeant
Major

Sergeant
Major
of the Army

Warrant
Officer 1

Chief Warrant
Officer 2

Chief Warrant
Officer 3

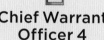
Chief Warrant
Officer 4

Chief Warrant
Officer 5

OFFICERS

Second
Lieutenant

First
Lieutenant

Captain

Major

Lieutenant
Colonel

Colonel

Brigadier
General

Major
General

Lieutenant
General

General

General
of the Army

An enlisted soldier starts out as a private.
The highest rank an officer can achieve is five-star general.

These are the seven core US Army values.

Loyalty
Duty
Respect
Selfless service
Honor
Integrity
Personal courage

Members of the US Army Parachute Team are called the Golden Knights. They perform precision free-fall demonstrations.